My Descending Moon

Miguelina Ramirez

Copyright © 2023 Miguelina Ramirez

All rights reserved. No part of this publication may be reproduced, distributed, or transmitted in any form or by any means, including photocopying, recording, or other electronic or mechanical methods, without the prior written permission of the author, except in the case of brief quotations embodied in critical reviews and certain other non-commercial uses permitted by copyright law.

My Descending Moon
Ramirez, Miguelina

miguelinaspoetry@gmail.com
www.miguelinaspoetry.com

ISBN 978-1-7389325-3-5 Hardcover
ISBN 978-1-7389325-2-8 Paperback
ISBN 978-1-7389325-1-1 eBook

Edited by Katie Beaton, Veneration
Cover Design by Miguelina Ramirez

The information is provided for entertainment and inspirational purposes only.

Printed and bound in Canada.

This book is dedicated to my mother, Cara.
Thank you for believing in my dreams.

Table of Contents

NEW MOON

SUBTLE GLOW 3
DIM 4
SEARCHING 5
DEPART 6
MISTREATED 7
BRUISES 8
INK 9
DARK SIDE 10
INNOCENT 11
EGO 12
FOREVER 13
WHISPERED 14
LOST 15
MOVIE STAR 16
CRYSTAL BALL 17
DIFFERENT LIGHT 18
TRUST 19
BROKEN STRINGS 20
AFFECTION 21

BUZZING 22
VICTIM 23
THE CARCASS 24
SALT 25
SIDE 26
UNDRESS 27
CONSISTENCY 28
INTEREST 29
SPACE 30
TEMPORARY 31
GO 32
LESSON 33
LET GO 34
CHASE 35
AGE 18 36
EASY 37
LOOSE CHANGE 38
ROOM 39
LOVE 40
NIGHT SKY 41
UNRAVEL 42
WISHFUL THINKING 43
CRACKS 44
DELICATE PAPER 45
MIND 46

REASON	47
ASHAMED	48
PAINT	49
SILENCE	50
FORGET	51
EMPTY	52
HIGH SCHOOL	53
YOUTH	54
PRESSURE	55
PIECE	56
SOFT LOVE	57
REGRETS	58
INNER CHILD	59
REWRITE	60
GROUNDED	61
MARATHON	62
EARTH	63
ANCESTORS	64
REPEATED BLOOMER	65
VIBRATION	66
FRESH START	67
HOPELESS ROMANTIC	68
ALONE	69
GENTLE STRANGER	70
CURVES	71

FALLING 72
FORBIDDEN FRUIT 73
REPLACEMENT 74
STRANGERS 75
HEARTBREAK 76
ENTRANCE 77
VELVET 78
AURORA 79

HALF MOON

MOON 83
FAULTS 84
ILLUSION 85
DEFAULT 86
DESTINATION 87
TOP HAT 88
INTERCEPTION 89
EXIT 90
CHOICE 91
WALK..92
LONELY HEART 93
TRUE LOVE 94
SECOND CHANCE 95
OLD NUMBER 96

VOICEMAIL	97
MAIN CHARACTER	98
ACTOR	99
HEARD	100
ALIGNMENT	101
FACE	102
ETERNAL LOOP	103
PAST CHAPTER	104
NEEDS	105
ENOUGH	106
DOMINO	107
THE VISIT	108
ENDLESS CYCLE	109
ENEMY	110
TASTE	111
NORM	112
STORM	113
PARALYZED	114
UNLOVABLE	115
UNFUNCTIONAL	116
TIMING	117
YOURS	118
SO GOOD	119
INDIE FILM	120
POTENTIAL	121

CONTROL	122
THE GENIE	123
WAITING	124
BETRAYAL	125
HYDRATION	126
J + M	127
OCEAN	128
POISON	129
SHORELINE	130
SURVIVOR	131
WRECKAGE	132
MAP	133
RUN AWAY	134
UNIVERSE	135

FULL MOON

TWO LOVERS	139
TWIN FLAME	140
HURRICANE	141
FAIRY TALE	142
EMOTIONS	143
BULLET	144
ADDICTION	145
SPREAD THIN	146

WOMANIZER	147
CHAOS	148
JEALOUSY	149
TUG-OF-WAR	150
WAVES	151
HUMAN	152
MISUNDERSTOOD	153
SPARK	154
INTIMATE HEARTS	155
THOUGHTS	156
TRUTH	157
PARTNER	158
GOLDEN	159
OPEN BOOK	160
EMBEDDED	161
COSMOS	162
CARVINGS	163
MYSELF	164
PAIN	165
POET	166
LIPS	167
EUPHORIC ROSE	168
LIMITS	169
PASSIONLESS	170
WORDS	171

TALK	172
FADE	173
WINNING NUMBERS	174
WISH YOU WELL	175
SUNSET	176
SEASONS	177
PERSON	178
DANCE	179
LAST KISS	180
LIFE	181
ASTRO CHARTS	182
FAMILIAR	183
SHELTER	184
MAGIC	185
COMFORT	186
PLACEMENT	187
EMBRACED	188
SOUL MATE	189
COFFEE	190
AUTUMN	191
WITHOUT YOU	192
DEPTHS	193
SEEN	194
HAIR	195
YEAR 25	196

Preface

I wrote *My Descending Moon* as a form of therapy. My puzzling thoughts found their voice among the pages. Unleashing generational pain from my heart, I allowed myself to share the stories I've often withheld with such passion. A hopeless romantic, I truly am, for I have trusted fully with my brittle heart, time and time again, spreading myself thin for the ones who didn't deserve my authentic soul.

My Descending Moon is the raw version of my truth, an eternal loop of love, pain, and sacrifice. A battle that was often fought in silence. The deception and betrayal were just lessons on my path to self-discovery.

My Descending Moon is my second poetry book, written after *My Euphoric Rose,* which was a collection of poetry centred on spiritual growth and enlightenment.

I hope you find clarity, peace, and self-love in my books, for I truly wrote them with the intention of bringing forward an awakening in you; a rebirth, let's call it. For you, my dears, have a purpose in this lifetime.

NEW MOON

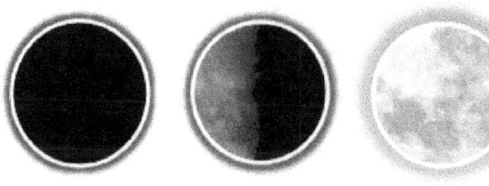

Miguelina Ramirez

SUBTLE GLOW

we match each other's energies
like the moon and the sun
you light the fire within me
allowing my subtle glow
to shine

DIM

dim the lights and allow me to fall into your sensitive soul
I long for your tender heart to be exposed in my arms for quite some time
and in a room full of outcasts, you are the main character in my story

Miguelina Ramirez

SEARCHING

I'm falling in love with your kind heart and
your love for life
you are the new moon that I've been searching for

DEPART

I can tell she's not fulfilling you by the way
your lips depart
when you speak about her essence
you lose a little bit of yourself in the dark

Miguelina Ramirez

MISTREATED

like the lotus flower, she flourished in
complete darkness
bleeding through her open wounds of
mistreated love, she always put herself last
she carries an invisible cut that always
tends to bleed
when she practices self-love

BRUISES

he stroked his ego and climaxed into her open
wounds, bruising her brittle heart
she took the beating
she believed this was how love was
supposed to feel
instead of healing
she let her fluorescent teardrops dance
the night away
slow dancing in the dark to numb her ongoing pain

Miguelina Ramirez

INK

I found therapy in my tattoos
inking when I felt at my lowest
I felt a sense of validation in the pain
too numb to express my deepest sorrows
with a stranger
I allowed him to break my skin's barrier and
create a masterpiece
for this was my therapy

DARK SIDE

he was ruled by the dark side of his moon
conflicted with his inner thoughts
she held on to him
hoping things would be different
wishing he was different

Miguelina Ramirez

INNOCENT

as genuine as your smile protrudes, the actions
were far from innocent
your laugh was far from innocent

EGO

your ego tends to talk when you're
around your friends

FOREVER

what was the point
in making me fall in love with you
when you knew I wasn't your forever?
you lit me up
just to leave me in the dark
my timid flame slowly burning out

WHISPERED

this is an illusion
your lusty eyes said it all
it will always be an illusion,
my heart whispered

LOST

getting lost in the shapes of my hips is what
you did best
the romance was just an illusion in this lustful
tale of deception

MOVIE STAR

a true born actor, he was
for he played many roles but himself

Miguelina Ramirez

CRYSTAL BALL

you started off dreamy
until your true palette resonated with your
superficial movements
the crystal ball was fooled by your truth, for you
roamed in the shadows

DIFFERENT LIGHT

trying to see you in a different light
is not working for the both of us

Miguelina Ramirez

TRUST

trust issues are formed when trust has been
broken, yet you didn't break mine,
you devoured it

BROKEN STRINGS

your smile was innocent, yet you played
me for a fool,
broke the core strings that connected our
decaying friendship

AFFECTION

all she ever asked for was some affection
but all you gave her was endless deception

BUZZING

the constant buzzing around your aura wasn't
enough to make you stop
mistreating your thoughts
for he disguised himself as sweet honey
but in the end, he was indeed the giant bee
that stung you

Miguelina Ramirez

VICTIM

our intimate hearts were the victim of such
a brutal betrayal

THE CARCASS

she unmasked her cloak and undid
her veil
hidden underneath
was her brittle carcass
coated with despair and deception
she roams in the hallow shadows for hours
lurking until she finds her next prey

SALT

you trusted me with your open wounds of
mistreated love
I distinguished myself as fine sugar so that
I could be close to you
aching for your approval to just love me
in my natural form

SIDE

he saw a side of her that she rarely shares
with others
and he was in love

UNDRESS

larger than life and introverted with your words
may you allow me to undress your thoughts
unravelling your complex layers
I can see your inner beauty piercing through
the surface
and it is refreshing, love

CONSISTENCY

as I unravelled the truth, it wasn't
about you or me
it was about the constant need to
feel something
the loneliness was just the dialogue
that disguised himself as a shadowy figure
following his victim everywhere
they may go
you were the closest thing to consistency for me

Miguelina Ramirez

INTEREST

I don't cry for you
I cry to cleanse my soul
I want to love myself the way you never did
the way you never could
jumping through obstacles for us
you sat and watched me
slowly lose interest in you

SPACE

the space between us was enough
to make you question if there was even
an us anymore
as though my kisses didn't matter to you,
nor my pain
I knew you wanted to run from this
conversation, I could see it in your eyes
but you found the strength to draw out the four
magic words I was dreading,
I need some space

TEMPORARY

our waiting period was supposed
to be temporary
it always was
we would break up just to get back together
the serotonin in our veins when we kissed for
the first time was addictive
a toxic trait that we indulged in a little too much
only this time was different
you were different

GO

I was begging you not to leave
when I should have been begging myself
to let you go

Miguelina Ramirez

LESSON

I have learned from my past hurt
to never trust a man that speaks poorly
about his exes
for they always seem to be the problem,
never him

LET GO

spread thin, I can't trust you
losing your self-control has always gotten the
best of you at times
but you're the reason I can't move on
I need to let you go

Miguelina Ramirez

CHASE

I no longer want to chase love
I want it to find me
want me
need me
feel me
squeeze me
but more importantly, love me
but in slow-motion

AGE 18

to be embraced by your warm grace,
you are my weakness
even though you crushed my spirit and
made me feel unimportant
at times, I fight back the tears and
the words to say I still love you
even though you found
it hard to love me
the way I needed you to
but we were kids
we didn't know any better
we mistook our happiness with false dreams
and filled it with emotional attachments
I wish to let you go, but a part of me will always
want you

Miguelina Ramirez

EASY

I need this time to be easy for me
I'm tired of always being the second choice
when it comes to your needs

LOOSE CHANGE

I can't afford love, as much as I want to buy
yours with my crippling heartstrings

Miguelina Ramirez

ROOM

I'll always make room for you
for our kind love, the subtle comfort of your
body pressed against my chest is truly magical

LOVE

I welcome you into the present
but please be gentle with me
I'm fragile from our past

Miguelina Ramirez

NIGHT SKY

take me back to the many nights
we spent embraced under the night sky
melting in each other's arms
wanting nothing more than for
time to stop

UNRAVEL

unravel my thoughts and unleash the whip
that silences
my tongue against my lips
sweet dreams echo in the wind
why is love parasitic to my mind
when I think of you?

Miguelina Ramirez

WISHFUL THINKING

I desire you in my dreams
that's the only time we may speak
only to be reminded of why we ended in
the first place

CRACKS

you hide your sorrows in between
the cracks of your dreams late at night
wondering why your vibration feels out of place

Miguelina Ramirez

DELICATE PAPER

how can you sleep so peacefully, knowing you
cause her such pain?
you snipped a piece of her essence with your
mighty scissor hands
knowing she was already delicate paper when
you met her
she spends many sleepless nights wondering why
it's so hard for someone to love her
the way she deserves
you crumple her words and throw out her pages
and as she glues herself together
she vows to never let her guard down,
for she is a mighty
book, and her story is yet to be told

MIND

you're speaking to me
but I don't hear you
consciously in my own world of sorrows
I sink deeper and deeper
into the void
becoming numb to my surroundings
I am paralyzed in my own mind

Miguelina Ramirez

REASON

I'm the reason why
I could never make them stay
and it hurts
why am I like this?
I always tend to drive away something that
feels good
my body rejects anything that feels good
I've become numb to feeling good

ASHAMED

I'm ashamed of the fact that I still
think about you
even though you weren't the best for me

Miguelina Ramirez

PAINT

I paint in our decaying storybook
of unfulfilled dreams
you lay on a single page
dripping in memories

SILENCE

I've become too attached to you
forgetting my own needs
afraid that you'll leave
if I take my focus off you
for a moment
I tend to suffer in silence
as I'm stuck in my own patterns
I can't seem to break free

Miguelina Ramirez

FORGET

in the midst of trying to forget you
I lose a piece of myself in the process

EMPTY

as I depart into space,
I ponder on our time together
and how I was naïve
to let a tall, empty glass drink my energy

Miguelina Ramirez

HIGH SCHOOL

my first love, my true love
high school was full of memories
we grew up together
you taught me how to drive
I taught you how to love
we experienced the highs of life
and the very lows
you now live engraved in my mind
I pull you out, now and then
and relive our precious moments
together

YOUTH

the flavours of my youth have a metallic taste
why is love so poisonous?

Miguelina Ramirez

PRESSURE

becoming comfortable with being alone
there is no pressure from the outside world
anymore

PIECE

my missing piece wasn't a person, nor an object
it was the missing piece inside of me that I had
to find and heal before I let anybody in

Miguelina Ramirez

SOFT LOVE

she was never in love with you
but with the way you treated her lonesome heart
you showed her a love that she'd never received
from her father
you valued her time, her dreams and desires
and she resented you for it
for she wasn't familiar with this soft love

REGRETS

stretch marks
tiger stripes
why do you hold me hostage?
bounding me to my clothes
I regret not jumping in the pool
when I was ten
fear of judgment
I sat on the sidelines
watching my schoolmates partake in their youth
making many excuses for
why I didn't want to swim
I wish that I had jumped in the pool

INNER CHILD

to heal my inner child trauma was often weary
she would always hide behind an invincible wall
shying away from crowds and blending into
backgrounds
she learned early on to pair love with fear
because to her, love wasn't feasible
and abandonment was always the end result
trust wounds wouldn't fully heal
she often neglected her self-worth
for it was crippled in the hands of her
relationships

REWRITE

I know I have to let you go
I need to fall in love with the version of myself
that's okay with being alone
I need to unfold the hands that were once
glued together
for I am no longer the unhealed version of myself
I will rewrite my beautiful story and hang it high
for the world to see

Miguelina Ramirez

GROUNDED

the clarity in my mind leads me to
where I'm truly needed and not mistreated,
for I'm always grounded

MARATHON

getting back to myself wasn't an easy process
what started off as a sprint, ended up as
a marathon
in finding my true authentic self
I welcomed the process greatly
suppressing my emotions wasn't going to
cut it anymore
for that had ruled all my past relationships
I had to come face-to-face with my inner
child trauma
and allow her to heal her past wounds

Miguelina Ramirez

EARTH

we were refugees to this planet
welcomed with open arms
Mother Earth showered us in her riches
coated us in everlasting love
yet as time excelled
we forgot our blessings and good fortunes
polluted her lungs with greed and hatred
for we were never satisfied within ourselves

ANCESTORS

as I stare at my reflection in the mirror
I see the eyes of my ancestors
and the many past lives that came before me
I see hope, love, pain, and sacrifice
swirling to the surface
and as wisdom breaks the glass
I bleed strength and courage
I shed the old me

Miguelina Ramirez

REPEATED BLOOMER

perfect in her anatomy, she stands tall
filled with many layers, she is a repeated bloomer
strong and mighty, she flourishes throughout
the seasons

VIBRATION

forward and never backward, I'm on a new
vibration, and it
feels good
toward the new me
I welcome
with open arms

Miguelina Ramirez

FRESH START

letting go of who I once was and starting fresh
with who I want to become

HOPELESS ROMANTIC

a hopeless romantic, she was
for she loved everything and anything that
walked into her lonely life

Miguelina Ramirez

ALONE

I hate feeling alone, it's been way too damn long
since I felt some real love
shining through my brittle wings
I always tend to set my exceptions low when it
comes to my needs

GENTLE STRANGER

he embodies a gentle demeanour
that radiates his presence
his soulful eyes are enough to make
you lose your thought mid-sentence
his lips will always quench my thirst
for he is a tall glass of water
I see the kindness in his smile
for he is a provider with those mighty hands
a feminist and a writer with his spoken words
his aura draws you in
I am hooked

Miguelina Ramirez

CURVES

he loves my curves unconditionally,
for they will one day
bring in life

FALLING

you fell for my smile
I fell for your heart
we both were falling from our past
relationship experiences
but this was different, you were different
so I thought

Miguelina Ramirez

FORBIDDEN FRUIT

the forbidden fruit was placed before us,
anticipating our sins
you looked deep into my eyes and knew this was
the beginning of our decaying love story

REPLACEMENT

all I can taste is the bitter words from your lips
when you say, *I found someone new*

Miguelina Ramirez

STRANGERS

strangers to friends
friends to lovers
you always had a way with words
now lovers to strangers
the silence takes me by my throat and chokes
the echoing space

HEARTBREAK

when heartbreak knocks at my door
I'll be silently waiting for its arrival
for I'm used to it by now, living a lonely life is all
that I've known, and it gives me comfort
I swallowed the bitter pill that awaits me
I was born a hopeless romantic in the
bottomless sea of the dating culture
for when heartbreak knocks at my door,
I will be waiting for their lips to depart
and hear the echoing words,
it's over

Miguelina Ramirez

ENTRANCE

deception and lustful dreams made their way
onto your horizon
you clapped at their entrance

VELVET

I used to wrap myself in blankets of velvet
I would romanticize my life like the movies
because my own life was lonely and pathetic
how can someone so put together be so lonely?
a hopeless romantic living in the dating culture
soaring through the seasons,
not a single rose was given
until a brown-haired boy
swept me off my feet
but he didn't deserve me
no one ever did
I needed to wake up and realize
there was no prince charming waiting for me
it was all an illusion in my fabricated dreams

Miguelina Ramirez

AURORA

my sweet aurora, you host the most beautiful
sunrises and sunsets
you coat my essence with hope and opportunity
the breath of life is embedded in you,
my sweet aurora
with the northern lights dancing many
nights away
and the echoing stars twinkling for many miles
I have been covered in blankets of warmth
and gratitude
you inspired my thoughts to form
and as the moon spoke to me on that crystal,
starry night
I knew this was just the beginning for me
as I breathed in your magic one last time
you hold a special place in my heart
my sweet aurora

HALF MOON

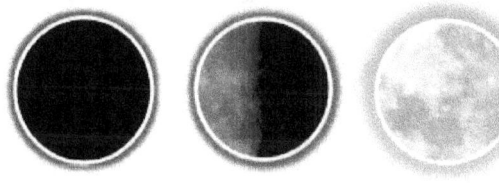

Miguelina Ramirez

MOON

my descending moon made its way unto you
soaring through the sky
you reached out your mighty hands to catch my
flaming hot pieces
scorching you at impact, yet you held on
because even at my lowest, you loved
every part of me
my sweet descending moon

FAULTS

a constant sadness follows him into every
relationship
one that he tries to conquer
for he is battling his own faults
the moon lights the way to his saving grace
for she knows he is in love

Miguelina Ramirez

ILLUSION

he unwraps her ridged layers and allows
her soul to sink into his
mounting her with lustful kisses
she believes in his actions
only to be deceived by them
he picks her up off the floor
only to bathe her in an illusion of decaying
flowers

DEFAULT

for touch is your love language
you made your presence known
pleasing your lovers is what you knew
excluding any emotional
attachments was your default

Miguelina Ramirez

DESTINATION

a Druid wizard, he was full of magic and deception
he drew me in with his deceiving eyes
his soul longed for my touch
my human connection was his
destination

TOP HAT

chaos walks down the street, wearing his top hat
he grins at the oncoming traffic
plotting his next move

Miguelina Ramirez

INTERCEPTION

you intercepted my life
like a moving vehicle
crossing the lanes into the unknown
I anticipated your arrival

EXIT

I never had an exit plan with you
I didn't think I would need one
I was so wrapped up in your milky eyes
I felt secure for the both of us
like it was us against the world
experiencing the highs of life
you felt like home
until I became the heat
trapped within your space
you decided you wanted the doors open
and so I escaped

CHOICE

I choose to close this door
that I've been holding open for you throughout
the years
hoping that one day, you would realize
I was the better choice

WALK

my heart went for a walk and never came back
packed a suitcase full of regret and marched
toward the mountains

Miguelina Ramirez

LONELY HEART

I'm always running from the pain
the pain that you caused
when you decided to deceive my lonely heart

TRUE LOVE

the key to her heart was buried underneath
the ocean floor
hoping that one day
it would be returned to her
by her true love

Miguelina Ramirez

SECOND CHANCE

if love comes back to you
hold it tight
kiss it goodnight
for it was always
meant to be

OLD NUMBER

sitting at the edge of my bed
I contemplated calling your old number
so that I could hear your gentle voice
one last time

VOICEMAIL

I left you a voicemail today
relieved at the fact that you didn't pick up
I scrambled to find the words to say
why wasn't I enough?
we were lovers connected by touch
the passion between us was enough to fill that void
inside of me
now that the distance is miles long
I struggle to cope
with the breakup

MAIN CHARACTER

build me a time machine and send me
back to when
we first met
the echoing voices in the distance, the winter air
on my rosy cheeks
your sweet face as you pulled me closer
it felt like a movie
and I was the main character

Miguelina Ramirez

ACTOR

the acting was prestigious
a five-star film
yet the script was not written
nonexistent

HEARD

you inspire me to write
for you are the pain lingering in my veins
wanting to be heard

ALIGNMENT

the stars were indeed aligned for our fate
you lost hope on the journey

FACE

if imperfect timing chose a face
it would wear yours, passionately

Miguelina Ramirez

ETERNAL LOOP

the moon couldn't emphasize with our love
for she had seen too many tragic love stories
throughout her time
it made her believe that heartbreak was
inevitable and true love was not achievable

PAST CHAPTER

when I'm alone with my thoughts, your face
always seems to make its way to me
drowning me with what-ifs
and as I'm far from your physical touch
I'm stuck on the chapter of us
I can't seem to move past it

Miguelina Ramirez

NEEDS

the subtle touch of her hand on your shoulder
silences the many voices in your head telling you
you're not good enough to fulfill her needs

ENOUGH

to be loved again is all that she ever wanted
she gave her heart in all her relationships,
but in the end, it wasn't enough
she was never enough

Miguelina Ramirez

DOMINO

he was the first domino piece
to start all of my next failed relationships

THE VISIT

depression visited me last night
he kissed my forehead
and filled my dreams with emotional pain
the aches carried on to the morning
bounding me to my bed
I felt hopeless
he tends to visit now and then
but last night, I wasn't prepared
I tried to break free of
the chains and shackles
but they were engraved within
I begged
please
let me go

Miguelina Ramirez

ENDLESS CYCLE

you work the 9-to-5
trying to find yourself in the world
living for the weekend, only to repeat
an endless cycle, you
wish for more in life

ENEMY

distraction was the enemy's way of bringing
tribulation
into the echoing space

Miguelina Ramirez

TASTE

you taste like regret
temptation running through our veins
how lustful of us to get to this place
you make me hate this version of myself
but I often crave your lips
I don't want to be just a warm body to you
but I love the way you taste

NORM

trying to match your words with your actions
I am misled, at times
disappointment is becoming the norm

Miguelina Ramirez

STORM

I would weather any storm that came between us
only to realize I was doing the loving for
the both of us
and it was weighing me down

PARALYZED

it's like I'm drowning from my own pain
unable to scream
I am paralyzed by my own surroundings
exhausted and defeated
I want it all to end

Miguelina Ramirez

UNLOVABLE

you make me feel numb
loving you is exhausting
you make me feel unlovable
but I still choose to stay
the silence between us has become
my comfort
restless in my thoughts
I am blinded by your existence

UNFUNCTIONAL

unlovable, that's how you make me feel at times
unfunctional without you in my life
how convenient for you

Miguelina Ramirez

TIMING

this regret now lives with him
to have met an incredible woman
with a precious heart, he truly was blessed
but it was the wrong timing for him
he broke his own heart
now lives with this regret

YOURS

it's been a while since I let my guard down
can you tell? I am emotionally exhausted
from fighting the urge to be yours

Miguelina Ramirez

SO GOOD

your love is like an open wound
as much as I want to heal from you
I can't help but press and poke
because this hurt never felt so good

INDIE FILM

our love story started out so innocently
like an indie film, we financed
our chapter together
through trials and tribulations
we were wide-eyed and full of hope
living in the moment

Miguelina Ramirez

POTENTIAL

he was in love with all the versions of me,
especially
the one where I wasn't at my best
for he saw my potential

CONTROL

I slept through the alarms and the constant
red flags
I thought if I did what I was told
you would love me the way
I've always loved you
but you just wanted something to control

Miguelina Ramirez

THE GENIE

he always gets what he wants
manifests his desires and lustful dreams
yet he can't achieve me
and it's slowly driving him mad

WAITING

you held on to me, waiting for something better to come along

Miguelina Ramirez

BETRAYAL

the betrayal was thinner than paper
the silence was lighter than air
for you were imprisoned in your own mind
desiring the lives of your victims at any cost

HYDRATION

I was water and he was a withering plant
longing for hydration
he kissed me with such passion

Miguelina Ramirez

J + M

stuck on you
stuck on us
you filled my empty cup
halfway then left

OCEAN

I'm drowning in us
overwhelmed with these
feelings
I accepted the love I thought I deserved
only for it to be polluted in turmoil

Miguelina Ramirez

POISON

you were monoxide and I was oxygen
grasping at my ribs, pleading with myself
to breathe
you locked me in and threw away the key

SHORELINE

I am drowning in you
can't you see?
the deep sea embraces my mighty waves
yet I can't feel our warm embrace
for I'm crippled by your touch

Miguelina Ramirez

SURVIVOR

the depression came and took you like a storm
blew down your mighty house built of bricks
the foundation withheld its standing
for you were a survivor

WRECKAGE

finding my missing piece among the wreckage
was exhausting and wearisome
I believed that if I looked hard enough and
found you
my past failed relationships wouldn't matter
anymore
it would all be magically erased
for you were my missing piece among
the wreckage
so I thought

Miguelina Ramirez

MAP

we were walking different paths, only for our coordinates
to have us meet in the middle of each other's lives
I throw away my map and start an adventure
with you
looking deep into your eyes
I am fond of this detour

RUN AWAY

run away with me to the unknown
I'll pack your suitcase full of aspirations
and optimism
our love will be the compass

Miguelina Ramirez

UNIVERSE

I'd travel through many galaxies to see you exist
you are part of my universe
indeed, my only universe

FULL MOON

Miguelina Ramirez

TWO LOVERS

naturally attracted to each other's vibrations
we were often getting lost in translation
but we didn't care what the world thought
of us, for we were two lovers
in love

TWIN FLAME

finding each other in the chaos
is what we do best
in a room full of souls
you are my
twin flame

Miguelina Ramirez

HURRICANE

he was a forceful wind trapped within
her hurricane
embracing her every move

FAIRY TALE

we laughed the night away
as you told me, you would make the move for us
we were already planning our life together
living in a fairy tale was all we ever did

Miguelina Ramirez

EMOTIONS

funny how one person can make you feel
so many emotions at once
and it's only been a week

BULLET

from your lips, the empty promises were
scorching
propelling over my ears
but I took the heat because
it was you
and this was us

Miguelina Ramirez

ADDICTION

he was kind to me when I was not so kind to myself
picking up my brittle pieces was what he did best
he was the passenger on my roller coaster
along for the ride
I anticipated how long he would last
and how much of my sorrows he could take
he slowly became my addiction

SPREAD THIN

chaotic minds
saying things we didn't mean
spreading our love thin
for each other

Miguelina Ramirez

WOMANIZER

a string of lovers is all he had
a womanizer
he cared for nothing but his own needs

CHAOS

creating chaos was your job description
conflicting your intimate relationships
was your expertise
for toxicity ruled your aura

Miguelina Ramirez

JEALOUSY

the jealousy was acidic
rotting each relationship, the victim
preoccupied

TUG-OF-WAR

let's be honest, this game of tug-of-war is
causing more harm than good
damaging our core strings
yet you continue to hold
your grip
out of fear of losing what we have

Miguelina Ramirez

WAVES

I often hold myself back with these decaying
emotions, but the waves
will always crash
if I stay with you
the endless excuses and the false hope,
the gaslighting
the crash is indeed inevitable
theses ties that held us together are slowing
breaking off
you need to let me go

HUMAN

inadequate, I am to you
folding my bondage into thin layers
I can't escape my humanness
why do we come with so much baggage?
chaotically driven egos, lustful desires
ecstasy running from our
veins
an earthquake of
desperation
altercations and unweathered dissimulation
polluting the lungs of our beloved Earth
taking up space, we are privileged
yet we can't stop
filling our mouths
our bellies will never be full
when it comes to the hungry ego

Miguelina Ramirez

MISUNDERSTOOD

I often ask myself why it is hard for someone
like you to love me
you fill me up just to tear me down
an unhealthy, whirling wave, I'm constantly
crashing from the highs

SPARK

all you ever did was distinguish my fire, burning
divinely bright
you couldn't stand my heat propelling
I would've been the match to spark the light in you
if you had just asked, but envy ruled your aura

Miguelina Ramirez

INTIMATE HEARTS

foolish hearts depart and ascend into the void
how could you be so reckless with her heart
when she opened her soul to you?

THOUGHTS

aggressive in my thoughts
I know you can see through me
is it normal to feel this exposed in your
presence?

Miguelina Ramirez

TRUTH

she was an observer
others saw her as an introverted masterpiece
always on display for the world to see
irreplaceable chinaware waiting to be admired
she was fragile yet untethered with her words
she saw the truth in people
as she quietly observed

PARTNER

she has never needed a partner
for she is what a partner needs
independent in her world
she is an empress
filled with exotic treasures
and desired by many

Miguelina Ramirez

GOLDEN

coffee bean caramel skin
she shines at her golden hour
dripping in rich honey
she is unforgettable
and unimaginable

OPEN BOOK

she undresses her soul in the moonlight,
for she is an open book
waiting to be read

Miguelina Ramirez

EMBEDDED

the crisp autumn air glistened in the wind
nature was always your second home
for the roots of earth were embedded in you

COSMOS

our story was written in the stars
for I was the stardust inside your eyes
and you were the cosmos in my Milky Way,
longing for attention

Miguelina Ramirez

CARVINGS

I was the shining pearl inside the oyster that you foolishly carved open

MYSELF

I choose myself in this lifetime
everyone else seems to be taken

Miguelina Ramirez

PAIN

and as I shifted my pain into power
and my shame into courage,
my heart walked back into my life
she gave me a hug
and praised my strength
bringing back souvenirs of hope and love
I welcomed her into my new space

POET

write me a love letter and send it to the stars
the moon will share our novel
a love story so rich in thought
treasured words one could only ponder
magic will ascend from our veins
our love will never have an end
our love will always live
in our Milky Way

Miguelina Ramirez

LIPS

he fell in love with my mind, my thoughtful words
he loved the way my tongue would hold
every vowel
before my lips would proudly depart

EUPHORIC ROSE

an empty high and a euphoric low
he broke my heart, so I wrote
as wisdom engraved itself in my veins
my euphoric rose blossomed
I showered my aura in words of affirmations
fell in love with my authentic beauty
for I truly was always enough

Miguelina Ramirez

LIMITS

the end has no face
it's the crippling pain we experience in silence
overlooking and analyzing our own character
too stunned to speak on our own faults
and even more staggering,
the fact
that they walked away so easily

PASSIONLESS

you stopped caring along the way
and when your kisses were no longer magical
the butterflies slowly died within me
our love became passionless
and you became a distant memory

WORDS

little did you know, your words followed me home
lingering in my ears
I try to brush them off
only for my mind to analyze your tune
making excuses on your behalf
I give in

TALK

all your love ever did
was talk

FADE

he didn't fight for her or their love
he let it fade into his empty cage of memories
for she was the one that got away

WINNING NUMBERS

I was your lottery ticket, yet you threw out the winning numbers

Miguelina Ramirez

WISH YOU WELL

I heard you got married this past month
while I was mourning the death of our memories
and future hopes that one day
it would be us against the world
I do wish you well

SUNSET

our ending was beautiful
like a sunset, your fluorescent colours appeared
and I held your gaze one last time
taking in your soulful beauty
because even though it didn't work out for us
you meant everything to me

Miguelina Ramirez

SEASONS

your love often lingers
through the seasons
when there is a subtleness to my surroundings
I'm reminded of you

PERSON

the time we spent can never be erased
I cherish the moments when we made
each other happy
for you were my person
even though
I was never yours

DANCE

even though I felt our love slowly fading away
I welcomed into my arms this slow dance
and rocked my hips to the beat of his heart
for this was our goodbye

LAST KISS

if I had known this would be our last kiss
I would have kissed you a little longer

Miguelina Ramirez

LIFE

once my eyelids begin to open
and the sunlight meets my smiling face
I know that you visited me last night
and as I shed a single tear of joy
I'm reminded of how life is truly
mystical
this one's for you
my sweet descending moon

ASTRO CHARTS

I hate when the summer ends
you always tend to run away
the summers were magic, filled with
endless laughter
exploring each other's astro charts
under the night sky, how lustful

Miguelina Ramirez

FAMILIAR

I'm loving your light, it twinkles in the night
letting your guard down
how beautiful
you talk about your passions
this feels all familiar
you feel familiar

SHELTER

clinching to your neck for shelter
I felt safe
the essence of the rain felt magical
only to coat us in sinful raindrops
we welcomed the cloudburst

Miguelina Ramirez

MAGIC

my worries dissolve
when I'm with you
for your kind eyes
see the magic in me

COMFORT

you make me love this version of myself
the one that goes to bed with a smile
and wakes up in a blanket of kisses
I have found my comfort in you

Miguelina Ramirez

PLACEMENT

there was never a place
where I truly felt safe
but between the crevices of your neck
I found my placement

EMBRACED

my soul journeyed many miles to be embraced
by your warm grace
for you are my weakness

Miguelina Ramirez

SOUL MATE

I want to feel you inside my soul
I want to drink your soft love
for you are my love language

COFFEE

you are my coffee
as I cling to my mug
I am energized by you
how did I get so lucky?
my hopes and my dreams swirl
into a cup, how refreshing
sipping on this morning coffee has never
tasted so sweet

Miguelina Ramirez

AUTUMN

you drove us to the beach
the fall air met our smiling faces
you were always a romantic gentleman around
this time

WITHOUT YOU

why does time fly when I'm with you?
it's because there's not a moment I want to spend
without you, he whispered

DEPTHS

can you allow me to undress your thoughts?
I want to get lost in the depths of you
the raw version of your truth

SEEN

his eyes spoke poetry
his lips wrote a novel
he made me feel seen
and that's all I ever wanted

Miguelina Ramirez

HAIR

you don't define me
but you are a big part of me
emotional wisdom
intertwined in every strand
I often wear my feelings and emotions in you
I take pride in how versatile you are
embracing your authentic beauty
a confidence that took years to emerge

YEAR 25

my magic number, how elegant of you to make your debut
I've been waiting to feel you
to hear your stories
to know you
25 feels liberating
I welcome your age with open arms
I know this is just the beginning for us
to be 25

www.ingramcontent.com/pod-product-compliance
Lightning Source LLC
Chambersburg PA
CBHW071435080526
44587CB00014B/1859